CHRISTLIKENESS IN MARRIAGE SERIES

Living Together

Happily Ever After

KEHINDE A. OSINOWO

Living Together Happily Ever After

© 2020 Kehinde A. Osinowo

The right of Kehinde A. Osinowo to be identified as author of this work has been asserted by him in accordance with the Copyright Law and Patent Act.

ISBN 978-978-986-926-8

Published by Christian Foundations (CHRISFO) Books
P. O. Box 7932 , Ikeja, Lagos
SALVATION HOUSE,
1-3, Salvation Street, Off Pipeline Road,
Baale Akinosi, Ajuwon-Akute,
(via Ojodu Berger)
Tel: 0803 301 1351
E-mail: christianfoundations88@yahoo.com
web: www.chrisfo.org

All Scriptures are from the New King James Version of the Holy Bible, except other wise stated.

Interior and Cover design by 'Tunji Abioye

Dedication

That Christ may be honoured
as the true Head
in the marriage and home of
JADESOLA and BOLUWATIFE.

To encourage and strengthen the hearts of all who
sincerely desire for CHRISTLIKENESS in their
marriages and home.

Acknowledgements

My heartfelt gratitude and prayers
- for the hard work of 'Tunji Abioye and all members of the Pastor's Office in putting this book together;
- the useful review and comments by members of the Pastor's Forum and;
- the contributions of other friends and family.

God bless you all, real good.

Contents

Introduction

This book is for the encouragement of all who desire for the christlike love, peace, harmony, fulfilment and joy in their marriages and homes: challenges in marriage and home, which sometimes have very disastrous and fatal consequences have been with the human race from the beginning.

The big problem now is that less and less people are aware of the solutions that God has made available for those challenges, talk less of appropriating them because of the increasing widespread distraction constituted by the ever enlarging human philosophies orchestrated by demonic arrangements for the eternal damnation of the human race.

Therefore, this book seeks to call attention back to the basic causes and **biblical cures** for those challenges that have continued to ravage homes, marriages and the lives of their members.

Interestingly, both the challenges and their solutions have their meeting point in JESUS as the only begotten Son of God.

"For God so loved the world that He gave His only begotten Son, that whoever believes in Him should not perish but have everlasting life." John 3:16

Lack of faith in this divine truth is the platform for both the institutionalised, personal and general problems being experienced in marriages and homes. Fortunately, the solution is very simple and divinely assured: it is to go back to faith in Jesus for the necessary rebuilding of foundations of your marriage and home on the love of God and the grace and truth of Jesus in the Bible.

"Come to Me, all you who labor and are heavy laden, and I will give you rest." Matthew 11:28

"For the law was given through Moses, but grace and truth came through Jesus Christ." John 1:17

And now, why are you still waiting? Arise and wholeheartedly come to Jesus for Christlikeness in your marriage and home!

Your servant for Christ's sake
Kehinde A. Osinowo

SECTION A

LAYING THE MARITAL FOUNDATIONS IN CHRIST

1

The Challenge Of Making The Right Choice

"So Adam gave names to all cattle, to the birds of the air, and to every beast of the field. But for Adam there was not found a helper comparable to him." Genesis 2:20

Not for Everybody

The position of your wife or husband cannot be occupied by any woman or man respectively. It is an office with pre-requisite qualifications.

That was why a spouse could not be found for Adam among the animals of the field and birds of the air. Notice that the fishes of the sea were not even considered! God had to make a new creature for Adam.

So it is with you as a child of God. As a son of God, you cannot marry just any woman – whether from the fields, the air or even the waters; your wife needs to be a new creature. And you, dear daughter of God, you need a new creature to be your husband.

"Therefore, if anyone is in Christ, he is a new creation; old things have passed away; behold, all things have become new." 2 Corinthians 5:17

That is the Basic Foundation

"For no other foundation can anyone lay than that which is laid, which is Jesus Christ." 1 Corinthians 3:11

As you can see in the Biblical Book of Genesis, the challenge of making the right choice of a wife is as old as the human race itself. Unfortunately, that problem has remained till the present age.

The point is this: choosing the right wife (or husband) is not a panacea for all marital problems. But not choosing the right spouse is like building a house on a faulty foundation.

"If the foundations are destroyed, what can the righteous do?" Psalms 11:3

You see; there are some unavoidable personality conflicts experienced in every marriage to adjust the respective individualities of the couple for a well fitted marital union. Where the couple is spiritually mismatched those adjusting frictions are more likely to be excessively hurtful and may become unduly prolonged or lead to different stages of disintegration.

This is the indispensable importance of the right choice of your spouse in Christ – to prevent avoidable crises. Yes, every marriage will have its own teething problems and growing maturity challenges but a couple matched in accordance with the Truth of Jesus is not likely to experience any level of marital collapse or avoidable pains.

"Therefore whoever hears these sayings of Mine, and does them, I will liken him to a wise man who built his house on the rock: and the rain descended, the floods came, and the winds blew and beat on that house; and it did not fall, for it was founded on the rock." Matthew 7:24-25

I feel compelled to clarify this point:
- Making the right choice of your spouse in

Christ is like raising solid and adequate foundation for your new house building;

- It will not exempt you from the hard work and expenses needed to complete, decorate and beautify that building inside and outside.
- But you would have saved yourself the painful and sometimes wasteful stress and expenses of repairing numerous and repeated cracks in your walls including the possibility of evacuation of the rubbles of the building if and when it eventually collapses

This is what wise Christian counsellors mean when they emphasise to intending couples that a broken courtship/engagement is a lot better than a divorce.

The Bible Also Warns

1. The Law of Moses forbids marital union with children from pagan nations
   "Nor shall you make marriages with them. You shall not give your daughter to their son, nor take their daughter for your son." Deuteronomy 7:3
   But why? So the Jews would not backslide and fall away from the mercy of God'
   "For they will turn your sons away from following

Me, to serve other gods; so the anger of the LORD will be aroused against you and destroy you suddenly." Deuteronomy 7:4

2. Even the Wisdom of Solomon could not exempt him from the consequence of his disobedience to this law:

   "But King Solomon loved many foreign women, as well as the daughter of Pharaoh: women of the Moabites, Ammonites, Edomites, Sidonians, and Hittites — from the nations of whom the LORD had said to the children of Israel, "You shall not intermarry with them, nor they with you. Surely they will turn away your hearts after their gods." Solomon clung to these in love.

   For it was so, when Solomon was old, that his wives turned his heart after other gods; and his heart was not loyal to the LORD his God, as was the heart of his father David." 1 Kings 11:1, 2, 4

3. The principle of this Old Testament law is still applicable in the Church of the New Testament.

a. The new testament eliminates the discrimination on the basis of nationality or race.

b. But your faith in Jesus now requires that you do

not expose yourself by marriage to the damaging influence of those who do not belong to Christ and their invisible demonic connections. *"Do not be unequally yoked together with unbelievers. For what fellowship has righteousness with lawlessness? And what communion has light with darkness? And what accord has Christ with Belial? Or what part has a believer with an unbeliever?"* 2 Corinthians 6:14-15

*"A wife is bound by law as long as her husband lives; but if her husband dies, she is at liberty to be married to whom she wishes, **only in the Lord.**"* 1 Corinthians 7:39

2

The Pains Of Making The Wrong Choice

"But there was no one like Ahab who sold himself to do wickedness in the sight of the LORD, because Jezebel his wife stirred him up." 1 Kings 21:25

Let us clarify a point: the goal of this book is Christlikeness in marriage; it is for those who believe that Jesus is the Son of God, the Saviour of mankind and they want to live their lives to please Him so that they can be glorified with Christ in eternity.

It is quite unfortunate that some of such people, who are true Christians and followers of Christ still experience long term traumas in their marriages.

Tragically, some get so emotionally hurt that they backslide or lose their faith in Christ entirely.

For many of such, the basic cause of their calamity is usually because they made the wrong choice of wife (or husband) and the first step towards that error is that they didn't ensure that their prospective spouse was a true Christian like them.

Although failing to ensure that your prospective spouse is a true Christian is not the only reason for making a wrong choice, it is the most basic and blatant reason for many a wrong choice of spouse.

Before I go on to discuss other basic factors to ensure the choice of the right spouse, let us warn ourselves of the pains of making the wrong choice of spouse.

From The Bible

1.   We have seen the example of King Solomon whose heart was turned away from the only true God to pagan idols by his many pagan wives. Unfortunately, this led to the defilement of the faith of Israel, its geographical disintegration and continuous wars between its

divided kingdoms (1 Kings 11:1-4)

2.   The bigger division (the Northern Kingdom) later had kings like Ahab who followed the heretic example of Solomon. His pagan wife, Jezebel, filled Israel with harlotry and witchcraft that started a process which culminated in the total captivity of its people. (1 Kings 21:25-26)

3.   Before Solomon was Samson, one of the judges of early Israel, a man of miraculous birth and special anointing to deliver Israel from the Philistines. Unfortunately, his own affair with a Philistine lady, contrary to God's word, led to the plucking of his eyes and his death with the enemies (Judges 16:4, 5, 16-21)

4.   *"Now Israel remained in Acacia Grove, and the people began to commit harlotry with the women of Moab. They invited the people to the sacrifices of their gods, and the people ate and bowed down to their gods. So Israel was joined to Baal of Peor, and the anger of the LORD was aroused against Israel."* Numbers 25:1-3

From Current Experiences

1. Many years ago, I became friends with Bro. A (a lecturer) and Bro. B (who was a senior lecturer in the same university). It was a season of socio-political upheavals and many lecturers could not get their salaries. Things became financially difficult in their homes. It was very clear that Bro. B's wife is a true child of God but the testimony of Bro. A's wife wasn't clear. Bro. B's wife went the extra mile to make her home socio-economically stable. Unfortunately, Bro. A's home became rancorous and we later heard rumours of his wife blatantly engaging in extra marital affairs and flaunting her proceeds before her husband.

2. I heard the story of a Philippine missionary, who committed suicide because his wife colluded with their daughter to marry an Islamic scholar.

3. I remember cases of Christian women that I came across in counselling, who went into marriage with nominal Christian men on the promise that the man would bring them

oversees after the wedding. Only to later discover that such men were already married to citizens of their countries of abode after the sisters rearranged their lives in their preparation to travel including resigning from their employment and sending their savings to the men.

Make Your Own Salvation Sure

Although there are other heretic steps taken by genuine Christians that lead them into wrong choices of spouse but this blatant error of being deceived into marriage by nominal Christians or those from other religious faith with a lame hope of changing them seems to be more with Christians who did not make sure of their own salvation before marriage.

Therefore the first step for you to ensure that you do not fall into marriage with a wrong choice is to make sure that you have a true and life changing relationship with Jesus.

Although, you may choose to rebel but a true

relationship with Jesus that is based on the word of God will enhance your capacity to discern deceivers when they come.

"Then Jesus spoke to them again, saying, "I am the light of the world. He who follows Me shall not walk in darkness, but have the light of life."" John 8:12

3

Other Contributory Factors

"Can two walk together, unless they are agreed?" Amos 3:3

There are other factors that make Christians to either fail or succeed in making the right marital choice.

They include:

i.   A clearly defined purpose for the marriage;

ii. Following your convictions (for as long as those convictions are in accordance with the Truth of Jesus in the Bible and your heart is sincerely opened to the promptings of the Holy Spirit);

iii.   Communication for unity of understanding;
iv.   Heartfelt and scriptural agreement;
v.   Parental consent.

Purpose of Marriage

One major negative consequence of the Fall of Man in the Garden of Eden is that the human nature became dysfunctional and one of the negative effects of that is that we are more prone to lose the purpose of creation and concentrate on benefits.

In the case of marriage, although some of those benefits have become virtually indispensable because of corruption of our flesh, all of them have the capacity to expose the soul to defilement, when taken out of the context of the purpose of the marriage, with the possibility of eventual loss of the soul to satanic manipulations, temptations and eternal damnation.

Talking biblically;
- In the secular sense, marriage was made for utility purpose (Gen. 2:15, 18);
- In the spiritual sense, marriage was made for

demonstration and fulfilment of the ministry of Christ, as the Son of God. (Eph. 5:30-32)

(This is why it cannot be over-emphasised that you have to cultivate a life transforming faith in Christ, fellowship with the Holy Spirit and obedience to the Truth of Jesus in the Bible before you make a choice of your spouse. You also need to ensure that your prospective spouse has been independently doing the same. Without that relationship with Christ, you can neither discern nor fulfil the purpose of God for your life, marriage, etc.)

Those marital benefits like:
- The pleasure of romance and sex;
- The honour of marital social status; especially for the ladies;
- The joy and warmth of companionship;
- The sense of belonging and/or ownership;
- The thrill of procreation and enlarging family, etc.

are good, godly, scripturally approved and desirable.

But in themselves, they do not constitute the

primary divine purpose of marriage. Depending on the spiritual maturity of the couple those benefits are meant to make the journey to divine purpose palatable and by that, encouraging perseverance.

It is like the pleasure derivable from the taste of well cooked food while the purpose of food is meant to be nutritional. Unfortunately, like all human phenomena, "junk food" is more common because we have been distracted from the purpose of food.

"All things are lawful for me, but all things are not helpful. All things are lawful for me, but I will not be brought under the power of any. Foods for the stomach and the stomach for foods, but God will destroy both it and them. Now the body is not for sexual immorality but for the Lord, and the Lord for the body." 1 Corinthians 6:12-13

The basic reason why God established the institution of marriage is to provide an appropriate and loyal human help to the man in the pursuit of his divine assignment.

Therefore, before a true Christian young man can

make the right choice of his spouse, he needs to cultivate the fellowship of the Holy Spirit (by meditating in the Bible, praying in the Spirit, receiving appropriate scriptural counsels, etc.) for the enlightenment of the eyes of his understanding to pursue his divine purpose by discerning his:

i.   Vocation – career that God wired him for and;

ii. Spiritual assignment on earth – his ministry in and through the church.

His vocation is the means by which he feeds to keep soul and body together and to raise finance and other necessary resources for the execution of his spiritual assignment.

It is his spiritual assignment that provides him the platform for spiritual growth, maturity and fulfilment of divine purpose.

"And He Himself gave some to be apostles, some prophets, some evangelists, and some pastors and teachers, for the equipping of the saints for the work of ministry, for the edifying of the body of Christ, till we all come to the unity of the faith and of the knowledge of the Son of God, to a perfect man, to the measure of the stature of the fullness of

*Christ; from whom the whole body, joined and knit together by **what every joint supplies**, according to the effective working by which every part does its share, causes growth of the body **for the edifying of itself** in love."* Ephesians 4:11-13, 16

Young man, it is your commitment to your spiritual assignment that will enable you to define the criteria by which you will discern that true Christian woman suitable to help you. It is not all genuine Christian ladies that can fit in as your own help meet.

A similar principle applies to you as well, young lady

- You cannot fit in as the rib of every true Christian young man with a godly vision;
- It is your own commitment to your own spiritual assignment that will enable you discern the man with whom you can flourish while at the same time you are facilitating his capacity to please God.

It is only then that your marriage can run on a joint vision with little or no reason for conflicts of interests, etc.

Follow Your Convictions

All that you will ever need for a prosperous and fulfilled life is released by the pursuit of your spiritual assignment.

Therefore, do not compromise your convictions of your criteria for making the marital choice because of either the pleasure of the flesh, fear of delay or a sense of dependence on man.

"Therefore do not be unwise, but understand what the will of the Lord is. And do not be drunk with wine, in which is dissipation; but be filled with the Spirit." Ephesians 5:17-18

Communicate Openly With Your Prospective Spouse

It is important that you are both on the same page with respect to the divine purpose and scriptural structure of your intended marriage and its home.
"But I want you to know that the head of every man is Christ, the head of woman is man, and the head of Christ

is God." 1 Corinthians 11:3

Heartfelt and Scriptural Agreement

Please do not force yourself into a compromised peace of conviction to enter into a marriage relationship. Do your spiritual, medical, physiological, emotional, temperamental, intellectual, social and physical due diligence to ensure that your conviction is truly scriptural and from God. Both of you must do your independent due diligence. None should either manipulate, force or depend on the other. Do not be ruled either by fear or pride.

"then I said, 'The Philistines will now come down on me at Gilgal, and I have not made supplication to the LORD.' Therefore I felt compelled, and offered a burnt offering." 1 Samuel 13:12

"Then Saul said to Samuel, "I have sinned, for I have transgressed the commandment of the LORD and your words, because I feared the people and obeyed their voice." 1 Samuel 15:24

4

Parental Consent

"Honor your father and mother," which is the first commandment with promise: "that it may be well with you and you may live long on the earth." Ephesians 6:2-3

A scripturally approved marriage is the result of the following two phenomena

i.   heartfelt and scripturally approved agreement between the bride and bridegroom to be united to fulfil the purpose of Christ

ii.   freewill consent and blessings of the parents from both sides.

In the Old Testament, the need for parental consent

superseded the agreement between the intending couple

"If her father utterly refuses to give her to him, he shall pay money according to the bride-price of virgins." Exodus 22:17

That Mosaic Law from the Old Testament was also confirmed as part of the principles of the Doctrine of Christ in the New Testament.

"So then both the father who gives his virgin daughter in marriage does well, and he who does not give her in marriage will do better." 1 Corinthians 7:38 (AMP)

It is this scripturally approved principle that is being independently corroborated or adopted in the ways that various cultures and traditions all over the world conduct their marital choice processes and wedding ceremonies e.g. till this present time, marriages arranged by parents independent of the couple are still very common in Asia and among Islamic people. Sometimes, the intending couples were betrothed to themselves while still in the wombs of their respective parents.

"For when Gentiles, who do not have the law, by nature

do the things in the law, these, although not having the law, are a law to themselves, who show the work of the law written in their hearts, their conscience also bearing witness, and between themselves their thoughts accusing or else excusing them)" Romans 2:14-15

This practice is foundational to the judeo-christian civilisation:

- It can be inferred in the biblical account of Abraham and his own father – Terah (Gen. 11:29-31);
- Abraham independently arranged Rebecca to become the wife of his son Isaac (Gen. 24);
- Isaac decided on where Jacob should marry from and;
- God blessed the independent choice of Laban to give his first daughter – Leah to Jacob as wife.

Parental Blessing

Although Isaac loved Esau more than Jacob, yet Esau's marriages were not blessed by his father (who preferred him) and mother because Esau disregarded both his mother and father in his marital choices.

"Esau saw that Isaac had blessed Jacob and sent him away to Padan Aram to take himself a wife from there, and that as he blessed him he gave him a charge, saying, "You shall not take a wife from the daughters of Canaan," and that Jacob had obeyed his father and his mother and had gone to Padan Aram. **Also Esau saw that the daughters of Canaan did not please his father Isaac.**" Genesis 28:6-8

"When Esau was forty years old, he took as wives Judith the daughter of Beeri the Hittite, and Basemath the daughter of Elon the Hittite. And they were a grief of mind to Isaac and Rebekah." Genesis 26:34-35

Life is a Continuum

Parental care should be a two way process

- Responsible parents give significant portions of their lives to care for their children until the children are able to stand on their own;

- God expects to use these children to take care of their parents when those parents become old and dependent.

    "But if any widow has children or grandchildren, let them first learn to show piety at home and to repay

their parents; for this is good and acceptable before God. But if anyone does not provide for his own, and especially for those of his household, he has denied the faith and is worse than an unbeliever." 1 Timothy 5:4, 8

This is also a psychological reason for children to give the opinion of their parents some good weight in making marital choices.

But There is More To It

For true Christian parents who take their parental responsibilities seriously, there may be a lot that God has revealed to them about the future of their children that those children might still not be matured enough to grasp, even at the point of marriage. Seeking the consent of their parents in marital choices would enable those children to appropriate the benefits of those revelations

- Consider Samson: he might have prevented his disastrous end, if he had submitted to his parents' independent position on his marriage *"Then his father and mother said to him, "Is there no woman among the daughters of your brethren, or among all my people, that you must go and get a wife from the uncircumcised Philistines?" And Samson said to his father, "Get her for me, for she pleases me well.""* Judges 14:3

- Also Jacob: maybe he would have wasted the grace of God in his life if not because he was restored to his father and obeyed him in his marital choices.

"Esau saw that Isaac had blessed Jacob and sent him away to Padan Aram to take himself a wife from there, and that as he blessed him he gave him a charge, saying, "You shall not take a wife from the daughters of Canaan," and that Jacob had obeyed his father and his mother and had gone to Padan Aram." Genesis 28:6-7

A Matter of Honour

It is also a way of honouring your father and mother in obedience to the commandment of God. So if a child spitefully ignores his parents' consent in the choice of his/her spouse:

- He/she rebels against the written commandment of God and;
- By so exposes his/her life and marriage to a

short life;
- And/or avoidable hindrances.

Grace in The New Testament

The biblical position remains the same in both the Old and New Testaments: it is parental responsibility to either get a bride for their son or to give their daughter in marriage.

However, the grace of redemption in the LORD Jesus has returned Christians into their original and intended relationship of God with mankind as FATHER.

"But as many as received Him, to them He gave the right to become children of God, to those who believe in His name" John 1:12

Therefore, for the Christian couple, the most important approval needed is from their Heavenly Father

*"A wife is bound by law as long as her husband lives; but f her husband dies, she is at liberty to be married to whom she wishes, **only in the Lord.**"* 1 Corinthians 7:39

This restored arrangement then brings appropriate scriptures into focus as follows:

a. The role of the father (parents) is to ensure that their children make their marital choices in accordance with the commandments of the Heavenly Father. In other words, responsible parents exercise their parental authority over the marital choices of their children as stewards of God over those children; not for their own self-satisfaction.

    "Behold, children are a heritage from the LORD, The fruit of the womb is a reward." Psalms 127:3

    "And these words which I command you today shall be in your heart. You shall teach them diligently to your children, and shall talk of them when you sit in your house, when you walk by the way, when you lie down, and when you rise up." Deuteronomy 6:6-7

b. Therefore, when a parent refuses to give his/her consent to the marital choice of their children contrary to the commandments of God, such parents disqualify themselves from the divine authority hierarchy and leaves the children with no other choice but to deal directly with the Heavenly Father.

    "When my father and my mother forsake me, then

the LORD will take care of me." Psalms 27:10
(This point is applicable only where the parental position is incontrovertibly contrary to specific principles of the Doctrines of Christ in the Bible)

c. Where the difference in the position of principle between the parents and the couple is a matter of opinion, it is expected that the couple would obey Eph. 6:2, 3 by accommodating their parents' preference in their final decision.

d. Giving honour to the parents does not always mean agreeing with them, especially where there is clear violation of any principle of Christ. In that instance, the couple must find other scripturally approved means of showing honour to their parents without yielding to that violation of Christ.

- It would require a sincere desire in the children to prove to their parents that they are highly valued and honoured

- It usually will include prayerfully and patiently waiting for God to change the parents' minds and;

- Might require efforts by the children to seek for the mediation of others respected by their parents.

SECTION B

PILLARS OF MARITAL HARMONY

5

A Journey Of Eternal Fulfilment

"This is a great mystery, but I speak concerning Christ and the church. Nevertheless let each one of you in particular so love his own wife as himself, and let the wife see that she respects her husband." Ephesians 5:32-33

Marriage is a Journey

Marriage is not an end in itself; it is only a means to an end

- It won't provide an escape route from the relationship problems you had with your mother
- Nor a solution to the "impossible" discipline and character demands of your father.

A man who didn't have either the humility or maturity to honour his "unreasonable mother" is most likely to find his relationship with his wife a lot more stressful. If he resisted his father's authority, he might not have developed the character to provide disciplined and balanced cover over his new home, especially his children.

So it is with a young woman who did not tolerate her mother, she might not find it convenient to play her role as a wise woman who builds her home and raise godly children. And if marriage is seen as a means of escape from her father and his home, she is likely to find a tougher version of her father in her husband.

It Is For Utility Purpose

Especially for the bride, marriage is not an automatic relief from baggage of psychological, temperamental and emotional challenges from the past. It is a place of work that will require your utmost spiritual, moral, emotional and physical diligence.

Marriage is for utility purpose; it is not constituted to care for the self-seeking weaknesses of the wife or the ego-driven demands of the husband. Rather it demands for their highest values.

This is why the word of God includes marriage in the list of "tools of purpose":

- Under the Law of Moses:

  "You shall not covet your neighbor's wife; and you shall not desire your neighbor's house, his field, his male servant, his female servant, his ox, his donkey, or anything that is your neighbor's.'" Deuteronomy 5:21

- Even under the grace of our LORD Jesus Christ:

  "So Jesus answered and said, "Assuredly, I say to you, there is no one who has left house or brothers or sisters or father or mother or wife or children or lands, for My sake and the gospel's." Mark 10:29

And What is The Purpose?

Answer: To become a son of God

"Then God said, "Let Us make man in Our image, according to Our likeness; let them have dominion over the fish of the sea, over the birds of the air, and over the

cattle, over all the earth and over every creeping thing thatcreeps on the earth." " Genesis 1:26

Man was originally made to become like God; that is, a son of God. That is the eternal purpose of creation: the solar system was created for the basic purpose of providing a conducive atmosphere in which God would develop a new specie of creation who would become like Him.

Let us remember that the image (i.e. the son) of God, the reality of which man was being developed to become is exemplified in Jesus Christ.
"Who being the brightness of His glory and the express image of His person, and upholding all things by the word of His power, when He had by Himself purged our sins, sat down at the right hand of the Majesty on high." Hebrews 1:3

"And we know that all things work together for good to those who love God, to those who are the called according to His purpose. For whom He foreknew, He also predestined to be conformed to the image of His Son, that He might be the firstborn among many brethren." Romans 8:28-29

"…till we all come to the unity of the faith and of the knowledge of the Son of God, to a perfect man, to the measure of the stature of the fullness of Christ" Ephesians 4:13

So, marriage was instituted as a back-up arrangement to help man fulfil God's original purpose for his creation.

"And the LORD God said, "It is not good that man should be alone; I will make him a helper comparable to him."" Genesis 2:18

It was a necessary addition to the other existing tools of purpose and the most eminent and intimate (Gen. 2:19, 20; Exod. 20:17; Matt. 19:5, 6)

A Union of Eternal Consequences

Marriage does not get made in heaven and it will not be needed in heaven. But its effects on the spiritual growth of each member of the union might either facilitate or hinder the fulfilment of his/her eternal worthiness.

"For in the resurrection they neither marry nor are given

in marriage, but are like angels of God in heaven."
Matthew 22:30

Although, marriage is made to enhance the ability of man to fulfil God's eternal purpose for him, (on the platform of which the wife also flourishes to fulfil her own eternal calling), it is unfortunate that the eternal destiny of some like Samson, Abigail, Solomon, Ahab, etc. were threatened by their marriages.

Therefore, both the bride and the bridegroom should be prepared and equipped to enter into marriage with a sober sense of duty and responsibility.

They must be ready for life-long continuous experience of personal adjustment for marital harmony and divine alignment.

It is a life-long experience of willingness to learn, realise, repent, be converted and be increasingly transformed into the image of Christ as a son of God.

The Pillars of Purpose

We have seen that marriage was instituted as part of

an arrangement to fulfil the mystery of Christ and His Church by which the members of the marital union and the children they raise may become true sons of God.

"So they said, "Believe on the Lord Jesus Christ, and you will be saved, you and your household."" Acts 16:31

Let us now look at the pillars of purpose i.e. factors that will facilitate the achievement of marital harmony, unity in the purpose of Christ and its fulfilment. They include:

1. Unity in the understanding of the purpose of their marriage
2. United agreement with scriptural hierarchy in their marriage and home
3. United acceptance that the marriage is for Christ.

6

Scripture Compliant Hierarchy

"…man was not made for woman but woman was made for man…" 1 Corinthians 11:9 (NLT)

The Woman Is Not Inferior

It appears that the widespread worldly philosophy of the so-called woman empowerment and the feminist sponsored calls in the UN for women equality have made discussion on divine hierarchy in marriage very sensitive.

Worsened by the recent upsurge of protests against Christian scriptural standards and call on governments to recognise groups like LGBT, etc., the scriptural arrangement for an orderly and harmonious structure in the marriage union has become misrepresented as oppressive to women. Nothing can be farther from the truth!

The Christian scripture does not consider the female gender to be inferior but different

a. she is compared to a weaker vessel (1 Peter 3:7)

i. a fact that has become increasingly attested to by science, weaker in muscle and not in intelligence and;

ii. very easily exploited by those who pretend to fight for the feminine equality and welfare.

b. But that same scripture requires that the husband must honour his wife.

c. with a warning that God won't answer the prayers of husbands who violate their wife's honour.

"Husbands, likewise, dwell with them with understanding, giving honor to the wife, as to the weaker vessel, and as being heirs together of the grace of life, that your prayers may not be hindered." 1 Peter 3:7

I am not aware of any other religion, tradition or

culture that comes remotely close to the height of honour on which the Christian scripture places the female gender.

More than that, the Christian scripture affirms the equality of the woman with man in Christ and before God.

"There is neither Jew nor Greek, there is neither slave nor free, there is neither male nor female; for you are all one in Christ Jesus." Galatians 3:28

To appreciate this fact, please take time to reflect on

- The scriptural description of the virtuous woman in Proverbs chapter 31;
- The counter – cultural prominence of women in the ministry of Christ while on earth and;
- The increasing stature and influence that the present day Church has afforded her women folks.

The Need For Hierarchy

As it is commonly said: *"there can't be two captains in charge of a ship"*.

That is why every proper organisation includes a structure and its hierarchy to ensure:

- Unity of command;
- Clear lines of communication;
- Division of labour;
- That offices are manned by the most appropriate skills;
- Responsibility and accountability.

It is also commonly acknowledged that the head of an organisation is not necessarily either the most knowledgeable or most intelligent. Usually, the head of a political government depends entirely on the expertise of his ministers and their departmental heads; same with technical companies, etc.

In all forms of organisation, the common factor in choosing the leader is "vision". The head is that person who received the vision and in the best position to articulate, supervise and pursue the execution of the vision.

In the marital union and its home organisiation, God gave the vision to the man and later created the woman to provide the help appropriately needed by the man. Just like a good king or elected head of a state seeks our people with appropriate qualifications and experience to help in handling the technicalities of his vision.

It is the man who receives the vision and in the position to ensure that the work is accomplished as originally intended.

"And see to it that you make them according to the pattern which was shown you on the mountain." Exodus 25:40

I believe that this is why man has been made head of his wife, home and children. It does not in any way denote inferiority for the woman.

In fact, when you study the definition of the virtuous woman in Proverbs 31, you would see that when the wife plays her roll well,

"The heart of her husband safely trusts her; so he will have no lack of gain. She does him good and not evil all the days of her life." Proverbs 31:11-12

There comes a time when her husband's recognition would be in reference to her own personality.

"Her husband is known in the gates, when he sits among the elders of the land. Give her of the fruit of her hands, and let her own works praise her in the gates." Proverbs 31:23, 31

Divine Hierarchy for Marriage

God established the institution of marriage with a clearly spelt out hierarchy:

"But I want you to know that the head of every man is Christ, the head of woman is man, and the head of Christ is God." 1 Corinthians 11:3

God, the Heavenly Father

Christ, the LORD and Saviour

Husband/Father

Wife/Mother

Home

Children

Under normal circumstances, every true Christian man has received a vison from God through Christ for his life, marriage, home, children, etc.

Therefore, his headship is not selfish aggrandizement but a sober responsibility to lovingly articulate, supervise and ensure the execution of that vision.

He is like any person under authority with a whole-hearted loyalty to Christ. It is in this context you have to interpete.
""If anyone comes to Me and does not hate his father and mother, wife and children, brothers and sisters, yes, and his own life also, he cannot be My disciple." Luke 14:26

Violation is Like Witchcraft and Idolatory

"For rebellion is as the sin of witchcraft, and stubbornness is as iniquity and idolatry. Because you have rejected the word of the LORD, He also has rejected you from being king." 1 Samuel 15:23

This divine hierarchy was first tested in the Garden of Eden and both our first father/husband and

mother/wife failed woefully. Eve, the wife violated the authority of her husband, Adam, who, unfortunately also violated his loyalty to God. This was the divine charge against the man:
"...Because you have heeded the voice of your wife, and have... (done)... which I commanded you...not (to do)..." Genesis 3:17

This was the beginning of witchcraft – Eve's rebellion against her husband's authority and idolatry – Adam's giving heed to another voice (Eve's) different and contrary to that of God.

Seeing the devastating consequences of this violation of Adam and Eve on all the human race, Satan discovered a very effective strategy to alienate mankind from the goodness, love, protection and blessings of God. (Gen. 3:1-24)

This is why Satan has set himself to influence the course of things in the world against the divine hierarchy in the marriage, leading to divided homes to which the Devil has easy access to plunder and lead their children astray against their divine destinies and well-being of the human race.

"in which you once walked according to the course of this world, according to the prince of the power of the air, the spirit who now works in the sons of disobedience, among whom also we all once conducted ourselves in the lusts of our flesh, fulfilling the desires of the flesh and of the mind, and were by nature children of wrath, just as the others."
Ephesians 2:2-3

Therefore, if you want the benevolent presence of God, divine guidance, help, marital harmony, fruitfulness and prosperity, seek to stay within the divine hierarchy.

7

It is All About Christ

"...as to the Lord;...Christ also loved..." Ephesians 5:25

The message of the Christian scripture is that the marital union is meant to demonstrate the relationship between Christ and His Church.

Husbands Hold Their Authority In Trust

"Husbands, love your wives, just as Christ also loved the church and gave Himself for her, that He might sanctify and cleanse her with the washing of water by the word, that He might present her to Himself a glorious church, not having spot or wrinkle or any such thing, but that she should be holy and without blemish." Ephesians 5:25-27

The husband should enter marriage with a clear mindset that will continually seek to make his authority a demonstration of the benevolence of Christ over his wife.

His goal should be to increasingly become able to relate to his wife the way that Christ relates to His Church. This authority, therefore consists of:

a.   Agape Love that is willing to make sacrifices and endure inconveniences in order to continuously and increasingly enhance the capacity of his wife to fulfil the pleasure of Christ in the marriage. This Christ's love is defined in 1 Corinthians 13:3-7

"And though I bestow all my goods to feed the poor, and though I give my body to be burned, but have not love, it profits me nothing. Love suffers long and is kind; love does not envy; love does not parade itself, is not puffed up; does not behave rudely, does not seek its own, is not provoked, thinks no evil; does not rejoice in iniquity, but rejoices in the truth; bears all things, believes all things, hopes all things, endures all things." 1 Corinthians 13:3-7

i.   it is deeper than material benefits and

ii.   not in selfish pleasures of the mind and flesh

iii. Rather, it is ready to suffer long to the extent that makes divorce an unlikely option;

iv. seeks for grace to quickly forgive and goes out of his way to make the atmosphere conducive for realization, repentance and reconciliation;

v. does not feel threatened by the good success and applause to his wife;

vi. But would rather encourage the atmosphere for the flourishing of his wife's diligence;

vii. does not seek to flaunt his contribution to his wife's success and praise in the public;

viii. does not have problem to rejoice under his wife's shadow whenever necessary;

ix. does not dishonour a respectful wife in public;

x. does not insist on his own opinion just to massage his ego; but always guided by his loyalty to Christ and His revealed will;

xi. he does not find it difficult to give room to sincere human frailties and so seek for improvement instead of retaliation;

xii. he does not either encourage or acquiesce with his wife's rebellion against the Truth of Christ;

xiii. he cultivates his capacity to bear and endure with his wife's sincere human inadequacies with true faith in God and hope for the best in his wife.

b.　　All these he does with sole aim of bringing his wife in line with the standards of Christ for her life and works

i.　　So, he teaches and trains her;

ii.　　Seeks to encourage and challenge her;

iii.　　Where necessary reprove and correct her;

iv.　　for instruction to righteousness in Christ

"All Scripture is given by inspiration of God, and is profitable for doctrine, for reproof, for correction, for instruction in righteousness." 2 Timothy 3:16

c.　　In all these, he wants his wife to be in such a relationship with Christ that would facilitate her ability to be his help-meet.

Also Wives Should Relate to Their Husbands as Representatives of Christ

"Wives, submit to your own husbands, as to the Lord. For the husband is head of the wife, as also Christ is head of the church; and He is the Savior of the body. Therefore, just as the church is subject to Christ, so let the wives be to their own husbands in everything." Ephesians 5:22-24

A wise woman would enter marriage with a mindset determined to submit to Christ in her husband.

Firstly, submission to her husband is the most basic evidence that the wife truly believes in God as omnipotent and that Christ is truly the LORD over all creation.

With this kind of genuine trust in God to watch her back, the truly Christian wife not only submits to her husband but flaunts that submission; even verbally

"For in this manner, in former times, the holy women who trusted in God also adorned themselves, being submissive to their own husbands, as Sarah obeyed Abraham, calling him lord, whose daughters you are if you do good and are not afraid with any terror." 1 Peter 3:5-6

Secondly, submission to her husband in accordance with the will of God and sincerely for the glory of Christ obligates God to vindicate that godly wife and where necessary show his disapproval of a violating husband.

"Husbands, likewise, dwell with them with understanding, giving honor to the wife, as to the weaker vessel, and as being heirs together of the grace of life, that your prayers may not be hindered." 1 Peter 3:7

No man can oppress or mishandle his godly and submissive wife and go scot-free. But this submission of the godly Christian woman to her Christian husband is meant to be:

i.   in everything
ii.   She is to submit to her husband, the exact way she would submit to Christ;
iii. She should relate to her husband at home and all aspects of her life as her head the way she confesses that Christ is her Head;
iv.   her husband gives her the physical opportunity to demonstrate whatever way she claims to revere Christ in her mind;
v.   she should look up to Christ to use her husband to save her body and so behave towards her husband in that light and expectation.

This is a major contribution to the harmony at home and fulfillment of the marriage:

- If the husband relates to his wife as if the real husband of his wife is Christ and that he only exists as the physical means by which Christ relates to his wife, such a husband will always seek to please Christ in his wife.

- The wife also wishing to please Christ in her husband will respect and submit to her husband as if he is Christ's representative.

The implication of the Christlike approach is that they must **independently and collectively** cultivate a two-way communication with Christ in His word and by His Spirit so that they can always discern the will of Christ.

""I am the true vine, and My Father is the vinedresser. Every branch in Me that does not bear fruit He takes away; and every branch that bears fruit He prunes, that it may bear more fruit. You are already clean because of the word which I have spoken to you. Abide in Me, and I in you. As the branch cannot bear fruit of itself, unless it abides in the vine, neither can you, unless you abide in Me. "I am the vine, you are the branches. He who abides in Me, and I in him, bears much fruit; for without Me you can do nothing. If anyone does not abide in Me, he is cast

out as a branch and is withered; and they gather them and throw them into the fire, and they are burned. If you abide in Me, and My words abide in you, you will ask what you desire, and it shall be done for you." John 15:1-7

8

When You Have Already Made The Wrong Choice

"…to console those who mourn in Zion…that they may be…planting of the LORD…" Isaiah 61:3

"…make the tree good and its fruit good…" Matthew 12:33

Divorce Does Not Automatically Solve the Problem

Statistics in the USA give the disappointing picture that:

- Divorce rate among couples in second marriage was about 60% compared to 50% among those in their first marriage
- Usually because those who left their first

marriage found out that their reasons for divorcing originally still existed in their new marriage; sometimes with more complications.

Those who did not jump out of the 2nd marriage were those who later learnt how to endure and sometimes adjust for a more conducive marital relationship and home atmosphere.

This is what they should have worked at in their first marriage.

God Hates Divorce

There are two grounds inferable in the New Testament as allowing divorce:

First is: adultery. But the general teaching and practice in the Church is that even this need not lead to divorce except the offender refuses to repent.

"And I say to you, whoever divorces his wife, except for sexual immorality, and marries another, commits adultery; and whoever marries her who is divorced commits adultery." Matthew 19:9

Second is: when one spouse persecutes the other

spouse because of his/her faith in Jesus. Even then, the scripture expects the persecuted spouse to endure and be longsuffering with the hope for the redemption of the offending spouse.

Divorce is allowed only when the offending spouse initiates it:

"But to the rest I, not the Lord, say: If any brother has a wife who does not believe, and she is willing to live with him, let him not divorce her. And a woman who has a husband who does not believe, if he is willing to live with her, let her not divorce him. For the unbelieving husband is sanctified by the wife, and the unbelieving wife is sanctified by the husband; otherwise your children would be unclean, but now they are holy. But if the unbeliever departs, let him depart; a brother or a sister is not under bondage in such cases. But God has called us to peace." 1 Corinthians 7:12-15

Outside of the aforementioned two grounds, the worst that is allowed is for a Christian spouse to separate him/herself for protective purpose until the offending issue is resolved; he/she is not expected to divorce.

"Now to the married I command, yet not I but the Lord: A wife is not to depart from her husband. But even if she does depart, let her remain unmarried or be reconciled to her husband. And a husband is not to divorce his wife." 1 Corinthians 7:10-11

Even in the Old Testament, the scripture takes exception to men who take advantage of their helpless wives:

"But did He not make them one, having a remnant of the Spirit? And why one? He seeks godly offspring. "Therefore take heed to your spirit, and let none deal treacherously with the wife of his youth. "For the LORD God of Israel says that He hates divorce, for it covers one's garment with violence," says the LORD of hosts. "Therefore take heed to your spirit, that you do not deal treacherously."" Malachi 2:15-16

Truth Be Told

A wrong marital choice is a commentary on the victim's understanding and/or practice of his/her faith in Christ.

Until such a victim identifies that error in the

practice of his/her faith and allows the Holy Spirit to help him correct it, he/she would continue to make wrong choices in any new relationship, whether marital, business, etc.

There are other heavy burdens likely to be experienced in marriages (and/or homes) built on scripturally wrong choices:

1. Except with proper counselling and a heart resolution to eagerly seek the face of the LORD for healing very early in the marriage, it might take quite a while in time and many traumatic episodes before the realization of the foundational error.

2. Unfortunately, even when the error is identified, it takes extra grace for the spouse who realises it to accept personal responsibility. The natural thing is to pass the blame to the other spouse.

3. Even when one spouse realizes, accepts personal responsibility and is eager to take steps for healing, the devil does extra work to keep his/her mate spiritually blind and unwilling to cooperate

Therefore, the bitter truth is that in many cases the

consequences of wrong marital choice constitute a life-long burden that must be endured.

"But he who endures to the end shall be saved." Matthew 24:13

A Mindset to Suffer for Christ

Therefore, one basic means of handling the life-long challenge of a marriage/home built on a wrong marital choice is to be ready to endure while looking up only to God for comfort and hope.

"But even if you do marry, you have not sinned; and if a virgin marries, she has not sinned. Nevertheless such will have trouble in the flesh, but I would spare you. But this I say, brethren, the time is short, so that from now on even those who have wives should be as though they had none, those who weep as though they did not weep, those who rejoice as though they did not rejoice, those who buy as though they did not possess, and those who use this world as not misusing it. For the form of this world is passing away." 1 Corinthians 7:28-31

What God Allows, He Uses

"And we know that all things work together for good to

those who love God, to those who are the called according to His purpose." Romans 8:28

One understanding that might encourage victims of wrong marital choice is that God's goal in all situation is redemptive.

- So, if the victim is a true child of God, it could be taken that God allowed that wrong choice for some redemptive purpose

- It might be for the victim, who is a true child of God, to use his/her Christian approach in that relationship to draw his/her mate into a genuine experience of redemption in Christ e.g. Hosea in the Bible.

Also, God could have allowed the wrong choice for the purpose of pruning the victim for a more fruitful service.

"Every branch in Me that does not bear fruit He takes away; and every branch that bears fruit He prunes, that it may bear more fruit." John 15:2

"My brethren, count it all joy when you fall into various trials, knowing that the testing of your faith produces patience. But let patience have its perfect work, that you

may be perfect and complete, lacking nothing." James 1:2-4

It might be God's way of preparing them to be counsellors who are more effective because they're able to empathise from their own experiences.

"Blessed be the God and Father of our Lord Jesus Christ, the Father of mercies and God of all comfort, who comforts us in all our tribulation, that we may be able to comfort those who are in any trouble, with the comfort with which we ourselves are comforted by God." 2 Corinthians 1:3-4

But It Is Not All Grim

Firstly, every trial has an expiry date even if that is at the point of death:

"No temptation has overtaken you except such as is common to man; but God is faithful, who will not allow you to be tempted beyond what you are able, but with the temptation will also make the way of escape, that you may be able to bear it." 1 Corinthians 10:13

Secondly, God is in the business of rebuilding the foundations of the repentant.

"Repent therefore and be converted, that your sins may be

blotted out, so that times of refreshing may come from the presence of the Lord" Acts 3:19

So, if as a child of God, you are in a marriage with a wrong choice, you need not lose hope:

- Know that God still loves you and wants to work all things for your good (Remember that it was when the Israelites were slaves in exile as a consequence of their rebellion against God's law that God gave them the promise of Jeremiah 29:11)
- What you need now is genuine repentance;
- And conversion
- Then you can peacefully, prayerfully and diligently wait on God for the promised times of refreshing.

(It is comforting to note that true repentance that is humble, broken hearted with a contrite spirit will always eventually be satisfied – Matt. 5:3-6)

Thirdly, I have come across the story of a true child of God who carelessly chose a deceiver as a husband. Although the home was quite traumatic for her but she held on in repentance, accepting responsibility for her own original rebellion and submitting herself to the pruning of the Holy Spirit. In due time, her husband and all his friends who collaborated to persecute her were convicted by her chastity and longsuffering; they all got converted to Christ and became her disciples.

I see some parallel in this story with the account of Leah, in the bible, who, though the first wife, was hated by her husband – Jacob. Her response was neither rebellious against her husband nor retaliatory against her rival wife. Rather she patiently waited on God while diligently learning and adjusting to win the heart of her husband.

God blessed her patience and diligent labours of faith by making her the mother of the pillars of faith including the lineage of Christ. He also honoured her godly feminine meekness of wisdom by making Jacob to eventually recognise Leah as his main wife and matriarch of Israel (Gen. 49:29-31).

In Summary

If you have already made the mistake of going into marriage with the wrong person, do not make a worse mistake by jumping out contrary to God's will in the scripture.

- Accept responsibility for your wrong choice and continue to patiently seek for God's mercy and forgiveness;
- Seek for grace for genuine repentance and conversion;
- Be humble to learn from your mistakes and be open minded to the Holy Spirit for continuous renewal of your mind and transformation of your character.
- Relate with your spouse as a project of redemption, healing and reconciliation.
- Be willing to cooperate with the Holy Spirit for the rebuilding of the foundations of your marriage and home.
- You may need the help of godly Christian counsellors
- But never remove your focus on God's faithfulness to fulfil His Word in your situation.

"And not only that, but we also glory in tribulations, knowing that tribulation produces perseverance; and perseverance, character; and character, hope. Now hope does not disappoint,

because the love of God has been poured out in our hearts by the Holy Spirit who was given to us."
Romans 5:3-5

SECTION C

PRACTICAL IMPLICATIONS

9

The Husband is Responsible

"For Adam was formed first, then Eve. And Adam was not deceived, but the woman being deceived, fell into transgression." 1 Timothy 2:13, 14

God Holds The Husband Responsible

Bro. Hassan had a prompting in his spirit to remove their daughter from the boarding house of the Federal Government girl's school she was in and turned her into day student. As part of giving honour to his wife, he sought for his wife's opinion. The wife opposed and later got one of the teachers to make Bro. Hassan change his mind. Although, Bro. Hassan didn't get a go-ahead in the spirit, he aligned with his wife's position and retained their daughter in the boarding house. Not long after that, the daughter began to misbehave and was forced out of the boarding house. At this stage, Bro. Hassan began to feel the prompting to remove their daughter from that school to another nearer home. Again, he did not obey that prompting in order to align with his wife. Unfortunately, their daughter's morals began to deteriorate so rapidly that she was expelled from the school, became quite wayward with much shame to the family and trauma to Bro. Hassan. By God's grace the girl came back to her senses and truly gave her life to Christ after many years of consequential waywardness. When she gave testimony of how and when she was introduced to bad friends, Bro. Hassan very sadly realised that that was when the Holy Spirit first prompted him to remove their daughter from boarding house. Bro. Hassan still regrets his unwillingness to hold himself responsible for making final decisions in matters relating to his marriage, home, children, etc. especially when he remembers how it has negatively affected some of their children, led to business losses and bad blood with extended relatives, etc.

The unwillingness of husbands to insist on their God-given convictions in the face of more convenient preferences by their wives or other members of the family is one of the most basic reasons for the increasing socio-economic and moral chaos, including marital disasters and wars all over the world.

It started with the first husband – Adam.

*"Then to Adam He said, "**Because you have heeded the voice of your wife**, and have eaten from the tree of which I commanded you, saying, 'You shall not eat of it': "Cursed is the ground for your sake; in toil you shall eat of it all the days of your life. Both thorns and thistles it shall bring forth for you, and you shall eat the herb of the field. In the sweat of your face you shall eat bread till you return to the ground, for out of it you were taken; for dust you are, and to dust you shall return.""* Genesis 3:17-19

Very sadly illustrated in the fatal judgement of God on Eli, his sons and lineage.

*"Then the LORD said to Samuel: "Behold, I will do something in Israel at which both ears of everyone who hears it will tingle. In that day I will perform against Eli all that I have spoken concerning his house, from beginning to end. For I have told him that I will judge his house forever for the iniquity which he knows, **because***

*his sons made themselves vile, and he **DID NOT RESTRAIN THEM.** And therefore I have sworn to the house of Eli that the iniquity of Eli's house shall not be atoned for by sacrifice or offering forever."*" 1 Sam. 3:11-14

So, when it comes to responsibility for obedience to God's word and/or will, the husband and his wife are not co-equal. The husband is the principal while his wife is his helper or assistant; they are not equal partners. Put it in another way, although men and women are equal, as souls before God but in marriage, they are not equal; the woman is called to help and support her husband, not to share authority with him.

Of course, a wise Christian man should normally consider the position of his wife before he finalises his decision but that decision must be his own.

Many times, wives might be more intuitive about certain matters and so hold more excellent opinions. It does not diminish the man's authority if he acknowledges his wife's better wisdom in the matter and therefore entirely adopts her position; only that it must be based on his own conviction.

A Mindset For Conflicting Independence Is Witchcraft

A godly wise woman should afford her husband the benefits of her opinion and responsibly make suggestions for improvement whenever necessary but she is not to disrespectfully teach or command her husband.

I have had to carefully counsel young women who complained that their husbands do not listen to them only to later realise that they meant that their husbands did not obey them.

What is Submission?

It means to give up your own position/opinion, even when it appears to you to be superior and to cheerfully pursue the position/opinion of another person, even though you think it is inferior to yours. There is no need for submission unless where there are differences in opinion. Unless when her husband's opinion contradicts the scriptures, a wise woman is meant to always submit to her husband in everything.

"Wives, likewise, be submissive to your own husbands,

that even if some do not obey the word, they, without a word, may be won by the conduct of their wives, when they observe your chaste conduct accompanied by fear." 1 Peter 3:1-2

In any case, a wise woman would always uphold her husband in prayers so that:

- He can always make decisions in accordance with the will of God and;
- Be humble enough to easily see and accept better wisdom from his wife or children, etc.

One of the fathers of faith in our nation was quoted as advising young Christian men not to marry any girl who does not always pray for at least one hour at a go. I believe that that advise was inspired by the Holy Spirit.

The reality is that:

- Women who find it difficult to submit to their spiritually responsible husbands are usually not prayerful;
- They are also not usually conversant with the Truth of Jesus in the Bible;
- They are usually more easily influenced by

high sounding worldly philosophies and traditional practices.

So they are usually unable to operate in faith but easily confused by the spirit of fear.

But It Is Not Enough To Submit

When a woman grudgingly goes along with her husband with a hope that he will fail while she might even be working on an alternative for herself behind his back, I define that attitude as "rebellious obedience"

A good woman would not have any serious challenge with submission if she is truly committed to the wellbeing of her marriage/home and fulfilment of her husband. Such a woman

- Might be the initiator of many of the productive actions at home; in which case the husband would see how they so well support his goals and fit into his own convictions;
- Would go extra mile to respectfully convince her husband of the benefits of her opinion to him and their home, whenever there is any

initial difference

The expectation of scriptures is for:

a. A wife to always do her husband good and not evil

    "Who can find a virtuous wife? For her worth is far above rubies. The heart of her husband safely trusts her; so he will have no lack of gain. She does him good and not evil all the days of her life." Proverbs 31:10-12

b. and to bring her husband to public honour and not disrepute

    "Her husband is known in the gates, when he sits among the elders of the land." Proverbs 31:23

What About the Woman's Vision

This usually requires that the wife is also spiritually ambitious with her own marital, home, family, career and ministry goals which she would have understandably merged together with her husband's to arrive at a joint goal for their marriage/home, family, business, ministry, etc. in which the wife flourishes and can be fulfilled in Christ.

God Does Not Author Confusion

He won't give a wife a vison that conflicts with her husband's and at the same time expects her to be his help meet.

What God does is to give every member of the family a sense of fulfilment in the same call

- The wife's vision to compliment her husband's while;
- The children's respective vision to enlarge the family joint goals.

10

Submitting To Your Own Husband

"Wives, submit to your own husbands, as to the Lord."
Ephesians 5:22

My Landlord Called His Wife "a Witch"

Many years ago, I learnt a very sober lesson from the landlord of the house in which I lived and his wife. The man went out on an appointment with a clear instruction that their only son should not go out until his return. While the man was away, his wife, for reasons best known to her, sent the boy out with his sister hoping they would come back before their father's arrival. Unfortunately, the bus in which the children went out had an accident and the boy died.

When the man came back and was told, he screamed so loud that all of us in the compound heard him accusing his wife of deliberating killing their only son for her coven.

They were Muslims and only God knows why the man didn't want the boy to go out and how he arrived at his conclusion. But in accordance with 1 Sam. 15:22, 23 rebellion is like the sin of witchcraft.

A Special Scriptural Injunction

In the language of New King James Version (NKJV) there are three levels at which the New Testament scriptures command submission in human relationships:

1.	Brotherly submission

	"Submitting to one another in the fear of God." Ephesians 5:21

a.	This submission does not include obedience and it is not a function of hierarchy;

b.	Rather, as further illustrated in Ephesians 4:2, 3 and Philippians 2:3, it is an injunction aimed at encouraging peaceful unity among the brethren through humble disposition that would normally give the others a sense of value.

c.   It is to be done in the fear of God

2.   Submission to spiritual leaders

"Obey those who rule over you, and be submissive, for they watch out for your souls, as those who must give account. Let them do so with joy and not with grief, for that would be unprofitable for you." Hebrews 13:17

a.   This submission is within the context of a hierarchy and requires obedience.

b.   It is meant for the benefit of the one who is called to submit so that he won't make it difficult for those set over him to develop him

c.   the beneficiaries of this submission are to be related with in recognition of their own capacities as spiritual leaders (see 1 Timothy 5:17; 1 Peter 5:5)

3.   The submission of the wife

"Wives, submit to your own husbands, as to the Lord. Therefore, just as the church is subject to Christ, so let the wives be to their own husbands in everything." Ephesians 5:22, 24

"Wives, likewise, be submissive to your own

husbands, that even if some do not obey the word, they, without a word, may be won by the conduct of their wives, when they observe your chaste conduct accompanied by fear." 1 Peter 3:1-2

a.   This is a unique type of submission where one person is divinely commanded to submit to another the way she submits to Christ Himself.

b.   Arguably, this scripture suggests that the wife's submission to her husband has to do with the "salvation of her body"

c.   It is within the context of a divine hierarchy and it requires obedience.

The Blessings of A Submissive Wife

By interpretation, proverbs Chapter 31 talks of a submissive wife and her many blessings including:

a.   vv11, 12 – she earns the confidence and trust of her husband – a basic ingredient of ease of understanding and harmony at home;

b.   v15 – a sense of worth and self-esteem that enhances her capacity to exercise, organise and delegate authority for the smooth running of the home;

c.   vv26, 27 (Prov. 14:1; 15:1) – calmness of spirit, wise words and gracious attitude that encourages unity, peace and manifest prosperity in her husband, home and children

d.   vv23, 28-31 – she is honoured by others – at home by her husband, children and household – and outside by the leaders at the gate

e.   vv30, 31 – above all she is honoured by God *""Many daughters have done well, but you excel them all." Charm is deceitful and beauty is passing, but a woman who fears the LORD, she shall be praised."* Proverbs 31:29-30

11

Sex, Money And Food

Sex, Money and Food

are generally seen as the culprits causing marital and home disharmony. I used to say that they affect the man only to the extent they show him respect or not.

But I have now seen that even the challenge of respect has a lot to do with communication.

Take the Example of Sex

It baffles many of us men that our wives still want to be toasted for sex. "After all we are married; is that not the deal?", a friend of mine was complaining that his wife was not forthcoming for kissing, caressing, etc. I answered: "do you know that some wives even threaten to sue their husbands for rape?"

A younger friend came to see me not long after their wedding. I played the double role of preacher at their wedding service and chairman at the reception. His wife was not responding to his sexual advances. I found that surprising given that his wife was previously quite sexually exposed. Anyway I told him a little I had learnt about toasting his wife for sex and for starting with his appropriate foreplay on the bed. The next time we spoke about the subject, although after a while, he was happy that his wife was now the one who usually initiated the sex move.

Many brethren who grew up in the Scripture Union (S.U) culture are not sexually exposed. So when they marry, it takes time for them to understand the need to help one another come into the mood before the bed performance.

This is why the growing trend of the Marriage Counselling Committee in many churches teaching intending couples about the modus operandi of their sexual relationship is commendable.

Anyway, it still boils down to the challenge of communication.

"Bro. Donald wanted deliverance from extra-marital affairs. So he explained that it was when he started to experience erectile dysfunction (ED) with his wife that he went out to prove his virility and got hooked. Further investigation revealed that his wife usually just lay on the bed like a log of wood when they had sex. Bro. Donald felt unwanted and gradually began to lose erection during the act and later as soon as he moved intimately closer to his wife."

So when another brother (Peter) came to share his problem of ED, I advised him to go and open up to his wife about his lack of emotional satisfaction after their sex act and let her know what he desires for during sex. He did; the wife showed gracious understanding and started making efforts to please her husband; his engine came back to full capacity.

I have since come to the conclusion that for many

sufferers, ED in men or frigidity in women is neither a spiritual attack nor a medical problem. It is often an emotional problem that can be resolved by friendly communication about sex between the husband and wife.

Many factors affect interest in sexual relationship between married couples including emotional and physical stress, ill-health, fear, sense of not being loved or genuinely wanted, financial insecurity, responsibility for children care, etc.

Most of them, if not all, can be honestly discussed and worked on together. Where necessary, the couple can together follow up with either medical or spiritual counselling and therapy, etc.

Food Can Also Be An Issue

Bimpe and Dele were love birds before they got married. It was Bimpe's fondness of Dele that made her follow Dele to Pentecostal Church. They married in Church and the union was blessed with sons and daughters. Unfortunately they are now separated. Although, they are not legally divorced, they live in separate places.

What led to that? Food! After many repeated complaints, the straw that broke the camel's back was that Bimpe did not serve Dele's relatives that visited with all the pieces of meat in the pot because she preserved a few for herself and her husband, Dele, when they would eat later. Dele couldn't be appeased; he was convinced that Bimpe hated his own people and not believing that his wife was repentant, he moved out and after a while succumbed to the call of nature with other women until he gave up faith completely.

Would the story not have been positively different if Bimpe had called to get her husband's advice to carry him along before leaving those pieces of meat behind? Maybe Dele would have provided a better alternative.

Other areas of food challenge include:
- Unsatisfactory quality or taste;
- Food not being ready in reasonable time.

With respect to quality or taste, my own opinion is that unless the inadequacy makes the food poisonous, eating the food in appreciation of his wife's sense of responsibility is the husband's way of reciprocating his wife's sacrifice by demonstrating the love of Christ. He can later at a more appropriate time talk things out with his wife. If necessary, he can help in the food preparation especially where the wife is always engaged in full-time employment.

Also, I learnt from a pastor friend that when my food is not ready in time, even after a period of marathon fasting, I should see it as a call for more time in prayers. That is another way of showing the love of Christ to our wives.

Wives Also Have Their Own Types Of Challenges With This Issue Of Food

- Many times, it is the wife that is the financial provider for the family. She goes out to bring in money and comes back home hungry only to find that her husband has just been waiting for her to come to prepare food. The love of Christ requires such a husband to help relieve his wife's stress and where necessary learn how to prepare food in readiness for his virtuous wife's return from work; especially where the man was idle for much of the day.

- In any case, better communication would likely ease any tension.

Joseph enjoys cooking and has many times in the past given his wife and children some special recipe as a pleasant surprise. But of recent, he started waiting for his wife to come back to prepare food including preventing the children from cooking in the absence of their mother. Mary, his wife became very upset and complained of her husband's new wicked approach knowing how stressful she usually came back home. Joseph's response was that he felt being taken for granted by Mary. All he wants is to feel that his wife responsibly thinks of his and the children's welfare before going out by giving the children instruction and letting him know the plans she had made for the feeding of the household in her absence.

Communication is powerful for harmony in marriage and household.

*"She rises also while it is still night and gives food to her household **and assigns tasks to her maids.**"* Proverbs 31:15 (AMP)

I do not know why some people say that African men do not help their wives to cook.

- I grew up in an illiterate African community. I grew up seeing my father helping my mother both in her market and in the kitchen.
- I remember a young couple in our neigbourhood; they washed their clothes together and handled house chores together.

In fact, like the Hebrews in Gen. 18:6, 7, certain aspects of food preparation are preserved for the men.

Anyway, whether African, American, Asian, Chinese or European, as a Christian husband, the love of Christ means that you sacrificially relieve your wife of stress, including in the kitchen.

The Challenge of Money

The man is the head of his wife as Christ is Head of the Church. Therefore, the welfare of both his wife, children and household is entirely his.

However, his wife is meant to be his help meet. So

both the man and wife should work out the best way to discharge his overall responsibility for the welfare of his household in all things.

That means that, considering their comparative advantages, they could both agree that God should supply all their financial resources through only one of the two; and that could be the wife.

I am not aware of any scripture that expressly holds the man responsible as the sole financial provider for his home:

- 1 Tim. 5:8 that is usually flaunted, when read in context, is talking to nephews of childless widows;
- Whereas, Prov. 31 can be objectively seen to encourage women to supply the financial needs of the home so that their husbands might be better able to concentrate on their spiritual assignments.

Even at that, a true Christian husband should still work hard in hand with his resourceful, virtuous wife as her protective cover and to ensure that the resources are channelled for the best of the household.

But a lazy and irresponsible spouse – whether husband or wife must be held accountable to 2 Thess. 3:10

"For even when we were with you, we commanded you this: If anyone will not work, neither shall he eat." 2 Thessalonians 3:10

Communication is Key

in any human relationship; more so in the marital union and the home. So let us look further into how to communicate for harmony and fulfilment.

12

Communicating Love, Peace And Hope

"The tongue of the wise uses knowledge rightly, but the mouth of fools pours forth foolishness." Proverbs 15:2

So whenever I think of communication between a husband, his wife and their home, some scriptures get highlighted in my head.

Genesis 2:25
"And they were both naked, the man and his wife, and were not ashamed."
True love is vulnerable and keeping no secret between yourselves as husbands and wives deal a deathly blow on Satan's ability to weave all sorts of imaginable lies around uncertainties

- Before marriage, come clean between yourselves; do not presume that something is not important for your spouse;
- Continue that practice of openness after wedding; it would help you sleep more easily and enhance trust;
- Where you think a matter is too heavy, seek for counsel and get the help of some godly elders that both of you respect, e.g. your pastor.

Matthew 7:7, 8

"Ask, and it will be given to you; seek, and you will find; knock, and it will be opened to you. For everyone who asks receives, and he who seeks finds, and to him who knocks it will be opened."

Marriage won't turn your spouse into a mind reader. So seek for the wisest way to let him/her know your pains, desires and be as specific as possible as to what help you need from him/her.

Proverbs 31:25, 26

"Strength and honor are her clothing; she shall rejoice in time to come. She opens her mouth with wisdom, and on her tongue is the law of kindness."

But ensure that your communication is done with

- Wisdom: i.e. however difficult the issue you want to discuss, set your mind for the help of the Holy Spirit to seek for an outcome of love, reconciliation, peace and hope. Mind your language, tone, time and place. Irrespective of how hurt you feel, always aim not to rob your spouse of his/her sense of value.

- And kindness: Kindness means adding value; treating your spouse better than he/she would have ordinarily deserved.

Colossians 3:15-17

*"And let the peace of God rule in your hearts, to which also you were called in one body; **and be thankful**. Let the word of Christ dwell in you richly in all wisdom, teaching and admonishing one another in psalms and hymns and spiritual songs, singing with grace in your hearts to the Lord. And whatever you do in word or deed, do all in the name of the Lord Jesus, giving thanks to God the Father through Him."*

Learn to cultivate a grateful heart not only towards God but especially to your spouse; also your children and other members of your household.

Bro. Jacob had a long struggle with bitterness towards his wife until he accepted the truth that the rewards of his sacrificial sense of responsibility towards his family will come from God and not necessarily from either his wife or any of his children. His hurts were about

- *His wife always complaining about him not giving her enough house allowance when she refused to work, preferring to be a full-time house wife. More than 90% of Bro. Jacob's monthly salary went through his wife for housekeeping, children's school fees, care of parents of both him and his wife, etc. The balance was hardly enough for his transportation to and from work. So he always came back home famished because he had no money to eat properly at work. His bitterness was based on the fact that he was transparent with his wife but she always retorted that the money only went through her and not for her.*

- *His children has been influenced by their mother to complain about their social life, when it is obvious that Bro. Jacob himself could not afford to participate in the social life he provided for them because he had to virtually sacrifice his life to meet those responsibilities.*

Virtuous Women Also Need Appreciation

I usually say that one thing that constrains me when I am about to be upset with my wife is that she risked her own life each time she went to labour to be delivered of our children.

Appreciate your wife, even if she is a full-time house wife. Many men need to realise that being a diligent house wife is one of the most stressful jobs available – if she wants to keep the house clean and neat, take good care of the children, including school runs and get meals ready in good time. If you find such a home, especially where they do not depend on maids, etc. the woman of the house must be disciplined, organized, diligent and persevering. Even where there are many house helps, it still requires a good dose of discipline, organisation and diligent supervision.

The challenge of thankfulness is that it requires some level of:
- Calmness of the spirit i.e. being at peace with God in your own heart;
- Contentment and trust in God for the future;
- Being conversant with the fear and Word of God.

Matthew 5:23, 24

"Therefore if you bring your gift to the altar, and there remember that your brother has something against you, leave your gift there before the altar, and go your way. First be reconciled to your brother, and then come and offer your gift."

I wish that I could tell you that if you kept all the foregoing, there will never be any misunderstanding between you and your spouse or children, etc. but that would not be true.

Because, we are not perfect in knowledge, Satan exploits our ignorance to tell us lies and cause misconception, mistrust, frustration and misunderstanding between us.

But it needs not become a source of strife:

- Always hold yourself responsible for the peace of your marriage and home (Rom. 12:18)
- This is as important as your other gifts or services to God.

Matthew 18:15-17

"Moreover if your brother sins against you, go and tell him his fault between you and him alone. If he hears you, you have gained your brother. But if he will not hear, take

with you one or two more, that by the mouth of two or three witnesses every word may be established. And if he refuses to hear them, tell it to the church. But if he refuses even to hear the church, let him be to you like a heathen and a tax collector."

Please go the whole hog. After you have prayed and taken steps, to the best of your ability for reconciliation and peace without any cooperation from your spouse (or children, etc. where appropriate), then seek for help, firstly from within the family unit and when necessary from mutually respected and scripture-compliant outsiders.

"Blessed is the man who walks not in the counsel of the ungodly, nor stands in the path of sinners, nor sits in the seat of the scornful; but his delight is in the law of the LORD, and in His law he meditates day and night."
Psalms 1:1-2

Proverbs 15:1, 2, 7
"A soft answer turns away wrath, but a harsh word stirs up anger. The tongue of the wise uses knowledge rightly, but the mouth of fools pours forth foolishness. The lips of the wise disperse knowledge, but the heart of the fool does not do so."

Communication is very complex; seek to learn and be open to improvement in your ways of communicating both verbally and otherwise: your tone of voice, your gesticulations, your face, etc.

Also, communication is spiritual. So seek to be continuously transformed in your heart, attitude, and life by renewing your mind in the word of God. It takes a heart that fears God and seeks to walk after His Spirit in the pursuit of Christlikeness to make the necessary sacrifices for love, peace, harmony and hope at home.

- Respond to angry barrage with soft, peace-seeking words;
- Do not just pour out your mind; you need "not spread your dirty clothes"; cultivate the Holy Spirit's fruit of self-control and restructure your speech in a godly peace-seeking manner
- Do not abuse your authority, rebuke with hope and give instructions that enhances sense of value.

Proverbs 14:1-3

"The wise woman builds her house, but the foolish pulls it

down with her hands. He who walks in his uprightness fears the LORD, but he who is perverse in his ways despises Him. In the mouth of a fool is a rod of pride, but the lips of the wise will preserve them."

Communication can be used to contribute to the up building or scattering of a marriage and/or home.

The solution is not to keep your feelings; that may eventually become more dangerous to your health and to the marriage and home.

Always seek for the grace to do the hard work of wisdom and kindness in your communication to promote love, peace, reconciliation, harmony and hope in your marriage and home.

Accept it as your own personal divine responsibi-lity; it is God who will reward you abundantly.

13

Making Christ The Head Indeed

"'...but their heart is far from Me." Matthew 15:8

The hymn: "Stand up! Stand up for Jesus" is relevant to this chapter's title. The first stanza and chorus is as follows:

> Stand up! stand up for Jesus!
>   Ye soldiers of the cross;
> Lift high His royal banner,
>   It must not suffer loss:
> From vict'ry unto vict'ry
>   His army shall He lead,
> Till every foe is vanquished
>   And Christ is Lord indeed.

Chorus
Stand up for Jesus
Ye soldiers of the cross;
Lift high His royal banner,
   It must not, it must not suffer loss.

That is a very appropriate song when we talk about making Christ the Head indeed in our homes. Why?

Firstly, because there are not many other social contacts where the transactions of the relationship are so personal and private as not only to get under the skin but also to touch the sensitive parts of the heart. The construct of its relationship makes the members so interdependent while it is not ordinarily easy to avoid one another as you could easily do in church or work place settings where you are not socially enforced to live together day and night. Unfortunately because of the human selfishness, this gives room to repetitive offenses, malice, prolonged resentment and deeper roots of bitterness.

Secondly, Satan doesn't miss such opportunities to entice to sin and death.

"But each one is tempted when he is drawn away by his own desires and enticed. Then, when desire has conceived, it gives birth to sin; and sin, when it is full-grown, brings forth death." James 1:14-15

Therefore, a resolution of heart to let Jesus Christ be the LORD indeed in your life and your home is required for the operation of that peace that passes understanding in your marriage and home.

Jesus is in His Word

So the only way that Jesus can be LORD indeed in your own life and in your home is when the Word of Jesus rules as the final authority in both.

Put it in another way, grace and peace come and are multiplied by the multiplication of the Word of God in the social environment of a life and/or home.
"Grace and peace be multiplied to you in the knowledge of God and of Jesus our Lord." 2 Peter 1:2

There Is No Special Harmony In Religion

This is how the LORD Jesus put it

"Hypocrites! Well did Isaiah prophesy about you, saying: 'These people draw near to Me with their mouth, and honor Me with their lips, but their heart is far from Me. And in vain they worship Me, teaching as doctrines the commandments of men.' " Matthew 15:7-9

Of course, I appreciate that especially as Christians, we do not wrestle against flesh and blood and that many times, the social and emotional challenges in our homes are directly or indirectly of diabolical origins. Even in that, it is our obedient faith to the revealed Word that breaks the yoke of the Enemy.
"And you shall know the truth, and the truth shall make you free." John 8:32

*"When evening had come, they brought to Him many who were demon-possessed. And He **cast out the spirits with a word**, and healed all who were sick, that it might be fulfilled which was spoken by Isaiah the prophet, saying: "He Himself took our infirmities and bore our sicknesses.""* Matthew 8:16-17

This Requires That You Ensure
1. That you consistently observe a personal quiet time.

a. this is a time you set apart on a daily basis, to study and meditate in the word of God without any distraction

b. it is a special time of fellowship with the Holy Spirit when He helps you search your inner thoughts leading you to conviction, repentance and transformation to become more like Christ. *"For the word of God is living and powerful, and sharper than any two-edged sword, piercing even to the division of soul and spirit, and of joints and marrow, and is a discerner of the thoughts and intents of the heart. And there is no creature hidden from His sight, but all things are naked and open to the eyes of Him to whom we must give account. "* Hebrews 4:12, 13

Bro. Hassan and Sis. Adebo have been married for more than two decades. For much of the time Sis. Adebo was not committed to meet Bro. Hassan's sexual needs. Although he brought it up occasionally, he was generally able to take it in his strides. So he became quite bothered when he noticed that he was becoming increasingly sexually vulnerable despite the fact that his wife was now becoming more responsive.

This became a major prayer point in his quiet time until one morning, during his quiet time, that the Holy Spirit impressed it on him that his sexual vulnerability was the fruit of his bitterness against his wife and that the way of escape was to become committed to forgiving his wife.

"Pursue peace with all people, and holiness, without which no one will see the Lord: looking carefully lest anyone fall short of the grace of God; lest any root of bitterness springing up cause trouble, and by this many become defiled; lest there be any fornicator or profane person like Esau, who for one morsel of food sold his birthright." Hebrews 12:14-16

2. That You Observe Daily Family Devotion in Your Home
a. It is by Family Devotion that you have opportunity to impact your family with the spiritual transformation you're experiencing in your own personal quiet time.
b. Family Devotion is not only for the family to pray together, but also to study, meditate, and apply the Word of God into their practical situations. It is also a time to arrive at united positions on current developments in the home

in general or their respective personal circumstances.

c. As a way of covering many areas of life and to learn from others' experiences within a controlled span of time during each day, it is recommended that Family Devotions can be based on Devotional Guides. There are many versions available today. In my family, we have always used Our Daily Bread (ODB) for its conciseness and time consciousness. As my wife and I began to have more control over our time, we added motivational guides like The Word For Today (TWFT). But I still use other guides in my own personal quiet time.

The Holy Spirit is so omnipresent that many times, these guides all deal with a particular issue of concern in our home with their respective perspectives.

3. That You and Your Family Belong to a Bible Based Living Church

a. It is important that you are convinced that it is the Holy Spirit who led you to the Church that you attend because that is your primary place of discipleship.

"You have not chosen Me, but I have chosen you and I have appointed and placed and purposefully planted you, so that you would go and bear fruit and keep on bearing, and that your fruit will remain and be lasting, so that whatever you ask of the Father in My name [as My representative] He may give to you." John 15:16 (AMP)

b. It is important that you and your family members participate in the same church to ensure unity of understanding and purpose without which the devil might cause spiritual dissensions

c. The Church is your primary place of discipleship, except for a few who are raised in genuine Christian homes, which are few and far between. It is from the church that you develop your capacities for Family Devotion and personal Quiet Time. Therefore, you and members of your household need to be mindful of the following responsibilities for you to maximize your discipleship potentials in the Church where God has planted you:

i. Do not carelessly and/or routinely forsake participation in the agreed fellowship meetings and programs of the church.

"And let us consider one another in order to stir up love and good works, not forsaking the assembling of ourselves together, as is the manner of some, but exhorting one another, and so much the more as you see the Day approaching." Hebrews 10:24-25

The devil is very apt in discouraging Christians from going to Church on the days that God has a word of healing, deliverance, breakthrough, etc. for them. It is the same devil that would later suggest to them that God has not answered their prayers. As the Yoruba adage says: "he encourages the thief to come to steal and arranges for the owner to catch the thief"

ii. Do not be a bench warmer or a "Sunday Sunday member". The Holy Spirit disciples you for Christ by giving you responsibilities through the Church Authority. A Christian who has no work or responsibility in his/her church is not likely to attain his/her discipleship potentials.

*"From whom the whole body, joined and knit together **by what every joint supplies**, according to the effective working **by which every part does its share**, causes growth of the body for the edifying of itself in love."* Ephesians 4:16

iii. You need to be financially committed to God in your church. Also train your children in the act of being faithful in giving tithes, offerings and other sacrificial financial contributions to finance the gospel through your church.

- Firstly it will help you to increasingly fix your heart on Christ.

  "For where your treasure is, there your heart will be also." Matthew 6:21

- And for your immediate material need, this is the platform for your blessings

  "But this I say: He who sows sparingly will also reap sparingly, and he who sows bountifully will also reap bountifully. So let each one give as he purposes in his heart, not grudgingly or of necessity; for God loves a cheerful giver. And God is able to make all grace abound toward you, that you, always having all sufficiency in all things, may have an abundance for every good work. As it is written: "He has dispersed abroad, He has given to the poor; His righteousness endures forever." 2 Corinthians 9:6-9

You can never out-give God!

14

Other Matters of Consequence

"But if any widow has children or grandchildren, let them first learn to show piety at home and to repay their parents; for this is good and acceptable before God." 1 Timothy 5:4

These are other types of pressure on the marital harmony as a result of responsibilities to or from third parties. Let us look at a few for examples:
1.   Tradition and culture
2.   Infertility
3.   Babysitting (*Omugwo*)
4.   Care of Parents

Tradition and Culture

In the 3rd (Annual) edition of Chrisfo Study Outlines with the title: Challenges of Our Time, some challenges categorized with Tradition and Culture include: Principalities and Powers, Anti-Christ, Family Ties, etc. Some relevant outlines from the CSO are:

i. that principalities and powers are invisible satanic agents adept in formulating schemes appropriate for ensnaring different types of people;

ii. Their goal is to lead mankind to hell fire

iii. They manipulate humans through thoughts, imaginations and inclinations enforced by corrupted temperaments, traditions and culture as well as the influence of family ties.

iv. Their manipulations are usually more pointed through cultural trends that contradict our Christian faith and are capable of luring away the Christian from under spiritual protection of the blood of Jesus e.g.

- Idolatrous practices in making marital choices, during wedding ceremonies and baby naming and/or dedication

- Occultic tendencies in handling sicknesses and

forging protection against suspected evils, etc. influence of superstitious beliefs about ...., way of salvation, reincarnation, etc.

My counsel is that Marriage Counselling Committees (MCC) in churches should include effectively life-transforming discussion on the related topics mentioned above in preparing the intending couple.

Many Christians do not know that apparently harmless traditions are capable of building satanic soul ties between them and ancestral spirits, etc. which can later be a source of disharmony and strange occurrences in the marriage and home of the careless Christian couple.

"lest Satan should take advantage of us; for we are not ignorant of his devices." 2 Corinthians 2:11

So what is the way of escape? Answer: *"...bringing every thought into captivity to the obedience of Christ"* 2 Cor. 10:5

This means that the couple should prayerfully develop the mindset to subject every thought, word, action, relationship or endeavor they are to undertake especially under the guise of the tradition and culture in the light of the Truth of Jesus in the Bible. Whenever there is any doubt as to approval by Christ they should desist:

"But he who doubts is condemned if he eats, because he does not eat from faith; for whatever is not from faith is sin." Romans 14:23

"Therefore, whether you eat or drink, or whatever you do, do all to the glory of God. Give no offense, either to the Jews or to the Greeks or to the church of God." 1 Corinthians 10:31-32

"Let the word of Christ dwell in you richly in all wisdom, teaching and admonishing one another in psalms and hymns and spiritual songs, singing with grace in your hearts to the Lord. And whatever you do in word or deed, do all in the name of the Lord Jesus, giving thanks to God the Father through Him." Colossians 3:16-17

The Christian is in a continuous spiritual warfare. Therefore, he /she must be circumspect.

"See then that you walk circumspectly, not as fools but as wise, redeeming the time, because the days are evil. Therefore do not be unwise, but understand what the will of the Lord is." Ephesians 5:15-17

It also means that your commitment to Christ as LORD must be total so that it cannot be assailed by any family ties.

"If anyone comes to Me and does not hate his father and mother, wife and children, brothers and sisters, yes, and his own life also, he cannot be My disciple. And whoever does not bear his cross and come after Me cannot be My disciple." Luke 14:26-27

Infertility

The original divine plan is for every couple to be fruitful and to multiply and I prophesy fulfilment of that scripture into every couple, family, home, etc. connected in any way to this book.

"Then God blessed them, and God said to them, "Be fruitful and multiply; fill the earth and subdue it; have dominion over the fish of the sea, over the birds of the air, and over every living thing that moves on the earth."" Genesis 1:28

"You shall not bow down to their gods, nor serve them, nor do according to their works; but you shall utterly overthrow them and completely break down their sacred pillars. So you shall serve the LORD your God, and He

will bless your bread and your water. And I will take sickness away from the midst of you. No one shall suffer miscarriage or be barren in your land; I will fulfill the number of your days. I will send My fear before you, I will cause confusion among all the people to whom you come, and will make all your enemies turn their backs to you."
Exodus 23:24-27

I doff my hat for true children of God who have endured infertility either as wife or husband and have remained committed and faithful for decades; those, in my opinion, are heroes of faith. Only that, it appears that not many Christians operate at that level of submission to Christ. Unfortunately, many Christians misbehave when they are faced with the challenge of infertility; some even give up their faith entirely. I have heard of Christians who backslide because they want male children. With advancement in medical science, many infertile couples have surmounted the challenge of infertility even at very old ages.

For those who might not be able to afford the cost of medically assisted childbirth, the option of legal adoption is becoming increasingly popular and has provided succor for Christian couples.

MCCs should introduce the option of legal adoption to intending couples not only as a way out of infertility but as means of meeting their desires for certain gender of children. Even without any medical challenge, legal adoption can be an evangelical means of eventually reducing street orchins.

This way, those couples interested would be guided to appropriate government departments as well as necessary considerations in their choice of babies for adoption in ways that prevent future avoidable regrets.

Legal adoption might be one way of God fulfilling Psalm 27:10
"When my father and my mother forsake me, then the LORD will take care of me."

Baby Sitting
Modupe's marriage practically collapsed after the arrival of their second child. Although, she didn't divorce her

husband but she and her two lovely children have practically moved back to her parents' home. The source of their problem is her husband's mother who insists that she must be the one to always baby sit for them. Since their new house is not big enough for their two respective mothers and Modupe does not feel so free to get all the help she needs from her mother-in-law, she gradually moved back to her mother where she was free to get all the help she needed especially when she went back to work.

The new couple should be taught to prayerfully consider and adopt a united position on this before it becomes a challenge.

For a Christian couple, where there is need for the mother(s) to help in child care, the first consideration is the spiritual influence that the mother(s) would bring into their new home. An idolatrous mother could initiate their baby to some strange spirit in their absence. Therefore, such mothers should be kept at arm's length. Subject to that situation the following factors should also be considered:

a.   under normal circumstances, it is the bride that needs to be cared for after childbirth and since she would usually feel freer with her own mother, her mother should be given priority in the earlier weeks when she might need more delicate care.

b. After that delicate period and if the two mothers are available and interested, then a mutually agreed time-table should be communicated and applied by the new couple as to when and for how long the two mothers come respectively.

c. It is wiser that each spouse should take it upon him/herself to explain the situation to his/her mother respectively.

Care of Parents

"Honor your father and mother," which is the first commandment with promise: "that it may be well with you and you may live long on the earth." Ephesians 6:2-3

When it comes to the matter of taking scripturally approved care of their parents, the couple needs to agree on the balance of the following two scriptural injunctions.

None of the couple (especially the husband) should subject their new home to the idiosyncrasies of his/her parents

"Therefore a man shall leave his father and mother and be joined to his wife, and they shall become one flesh." Genesis 2:24

But that does not absolve them from the joint responsibility of taking good care of their parents.

"But if any widow has children or grandchildren, let them first learn to show piety at home and to repay their parents; for this is good and acceptable before God." 1 Timothy 5:4

The right mindset is when the new wife and her husband sincerely resolve that they now each have two pairs of parents and work hard to make that a reality. That way, it should become increasingly easier to both jointly take good care of both parents with very little or no partiality.

15

Dealing With An Unreasonable Spouse

❦

"And that we may be delivered from unreasonable and wicked men; for not all have faith." 2 Thessalonians 3:2

Who is an Unreasonable Spouse?

"Finally, brethren, pray for us, that the word of the Lord may run swiftly and be glorified, just as it is with you, and that we may be delivered from unreasonable and wicked men; for not all have faith. But the Lord is faithful, who will establish you and guard you from the evil one." 2 Thessalonians 3:1-3

For a true child of God who is sincerely seeking to be a true disciple of Christ by always living his/her life in accordance with the principles of the Doctrine of Christ in the Bible, he/she has an unreasonable spouse, when that spouse's perspective of life is practically contrary and has no commitment to work at arriving at the same perspective in accordance with the Bible.

a.   The unreasonable spouse usually has problems with the way his/her wife/husband seeks to practice the faith that they both profess.

b.   The unreasonable spouse does not quickly yield to the word of God and does not have a sense of responsibility to glorify such word.

c.   Being controlled by fear and/or unbelief, he/she is usually neither able to trust God nor take the risk required to obey spiritually inspired instructions.

d.   When the unreasonable spouse is unwilling to grow in grace and faith, he/she usually begins to pretend, keep unnecessary secrets, breaks trust, makes the marital environment increasingly difficult to manage, easily stressed and irritable because of unspoken inner conflicts and may become unduly self-defensive and bitter.

e.   Unreasonableness in a marital union would

usually lead to various degrees of wickedness, including:

i.   all forms of violence with emphasis on physical violence;

ii.   various levels of starvations of sex, food, etc.

iii.   Spiritual and sexual infidelity;

iv.   thereby exposing the home to demonic activities;

v.   including curses, ill-favour, avoidable failures, loss of opportunities, etc.

There Is Always a Way of Escape

"Therefore let him who thinks he stands take heed lest he fall. No temptation has overtaken you except such as is common to man; but God is faithful, who will not allow you to be tempted beyond what you are able, but with the temptation will also make the way of escape, that you may be able to bear it. Therefore, my beloved, flee from idolatry." 1 Corinthians 10:12-14

Violence in Marriage/Home

It could be verbal, emotional or physical. Physical violence is the most talked about because of its inherent risk of major physiological damages or actual death.

There are newspapers' reports of physical violence by both male and female spouses like a woman cutting off her husband's genitals while he was asleep. However, the more common is physical violence by husbands.

My advice is for the victim to separate him/herself from the environment of danger until there is enough guarantee for his/her safety.

My niece was taken away from her husband's house because she had been physically assaulted by her husband even when she was with an advanced pregnancy. By the time my attention was called by the young man for mediation, my sister – his mother-in-law had already decided that the marriage should be ended; only for the young man to accept financial responsibility for the care of their small children. I advised my sister not to encourage her daughter into divorce contrary to God's commandment. Also not to put the young lady into sexual temptation by keeping her away from her husband. Rather, her husband should be "marrying her in her parent's house" until there is adequate arrangements for her safety.

A point to note however is that in many cases to which I have been called to intervene, there was usually a problem of actual or suspected infidelity by the wife behind the husband's violent frustration. The same type of frustration is usually behind the verbal or emotional violence of the wife.

So while the violent spouse is being worked on for better self-control, the victim must also be helped to repent of his/her cause of violent reactions.

Spiritual Exposure of the Home

Usually a product of spiritual disharmony.

"But if you have bitter envy and self-seeking in your hearts, do not boast and lie against the truth. This wisdom does not descend from above, but is earthly, sensual, demonic. For where envy and self-seeking exist, confusion and every evil thing are there." James 3:14-16

The first step to solution is for the victim to seek for

reconciliation and harmony.

"Moreover if your brother sins against you, go and tell him his fault between you and him alone. If he hears you, you have gained your brother. But if he will not hear, take with you one or two more, that by the mouth of two or three witnesses every word may be established. And if he refuses to hear them, tell it to the church. But if he refuses even to hear the church, let him be to you like a heathen and a tax collector." Matthew 18:15-17

But where the unreasonable spouse is unwilling to cooperate, the victim must take steps for the deliverance, breakthrough and protection of his/her life and those of the children.

"Do not trust in a friend; do not put your confidence in a companion; **guard the doors of your mouth from her who lies in your bosom.** *For son dishonors father, daughter rises against her mother, daughter-in-law against her mother-in-law; a man's enemies are the men of his own household. Therefore I will look to the LORD; I will wait for the God of my salvation; my God will hear me."* Micah 7:5-7

Sometimes, Physical Separation is Necessary
a.   Especially when there is physical violence.

A case was widely reported in the media of a man who was stabbed to death by his wife. The wife accused her husband of infidelity and threatened to kill him; she became violent. The neighbours called in the police who tried to settle the matter. The neighbours who observed the bitterness of the wife advised the man not to stay in the same room/house with his wife. But he felt the matter was settled and slept on the same bed with intention to calm his wife. Unfortunately, he didn't live to tell the story. He should have gone to sleep outside or locked himself in a separate room.

b.   **Even in the case of spiritual exposure**

I have come across cases of people who found themselves under different kinds of spiritual oppression until they moved to a different room from their spouses. In one particular case, he testified that he was more able to pray through and given secrets of spiritual problems in his home and how to deal with them victoriously.

Unfortunately, Only Divorce Resolves Some Cases

Firstly, let us remind ourselves that God hates divorce

"For the LORD God of Israel says that He hates divorce, for it covers one's garment with violence," says the LORD of hosts. "Therefore take heed to your spirit, that you do not deal treacherously." Malachi 2:16

Anyway, divorce should be avoided by the true child of God as much as it depends on him/her. However, he/she might have no other option when the unreasonable spouse pushes the true child of God to the wall. In such a case, the Bible allows divorce and remarriage in order to prevent avoidable sexual immorality.

Only two situations come under such permission

a. When the unreasonable spouse flaunts his/her adultery without repentance.
    "And I say to you, whoever divorces his wife, except for sexual immorality, and marries another, commits adultery; and whoever marries her who is divorced commits adultery." Matthew 19:9

b. when the unreasonable spouse rejects or sends the child of God out of his/her marriage because of the gospel
    "But if the unbeliever departs, let him depart; a brother or a sister is not under bondage in such

cases. But God has called us to peace." 1 Corinthians 7:15

God is Not a Taskmaster

As with all commandments of God, the principles of Christlikeness do not turn marriage into an avoidable albatross on the neck of a true child of God who seeks to please God.

"For this is the love of God, that we keep His commandments. And His commandments are not burdensome." 1 John 5:3

16
Eternity in View

"For this reason I bow my knees to the Father of our Lord Jesus Christ, from whom the whole family in heaven and earth is named." Ephesians 3:14-15

There Is An Eternal Role For You And Your Family
When I read between the lines in Dan. 12:9, 13; Eph. 3:14, 15 (as stated above); Rev. 7:4, 8, 9 and 22:3, I see that God has an eternal service role for His human servants as individuals, families, tribes, languages, nations, etc.

"And he said, "Go your way, Daniel, for the words are closed up and sealed till the time of the end. "But you, go

your way till the end; for you shall rest, and will arise to your inheritance at the end of the days."" Daniel 12:9, 13

"And I heard the number of those who were sealed. One hundred and forty-four thousand of all the tribes of the children of Israel were sealed: of the tribe of Zebulun twelve thousand were sealed...After these things I looked, and behold, a great multitude which no one could number, of all nations, tribes, peoples, and tongues, standing before the throne and before the Lamb, clothed with white robes, with palm branches in their hands" Revelation 7:4 ,9

*"And there shall be no more curse, but the throne of God and of the Lamb shall be in it, and **His servants shall serve Him**."* Revelation 22:3

Therefore the new couple should start their new home with the understanding and resolution of heart to fit into their own divine destiny.

This means that:

a.   They should accept responsibility by the grace of God to bring each of their children and every member of their home into a saving knowledge of Christ

b. They should see to it that each member of their home has a responsibility in the church by which they can be discipled in Christ.

"And He Himself gave some to be apostles, some prophets, some evangelists, and some pastors and teachers, for the equipping of the saints for the work of ministry, for the edifying of the body of Christ, till we all come to the unity of the faith and of the knowledge of the Son of God, to a perfect man, to the measure of the stature of the fullness of Christ." Ephesians 4:11-13

c. There should be a unity of purpose in Christ among the members of the family:

i. the wife should be a helpmeet to her husband. In other words, their respective works for God should be productively complimentary and NOT conflicting.

ii. While the respective works of the children should be such as to expand the role of the family in the Church and neither to ignore or unwittingly oppose it.

This Unity of Purpose is Important to God

a. It determined the position of father Abraham with God

    "And the LORD said, "Shall I hide from Abraham what I am doing, since Abraham shall surely become a great and mighty nation, and all the nations of the earth shall be blessed in him? For I have known him, in order that he may command his children and his household after him, that they keep the way of the LORD, to do righteousness and justice, that the LORD may bring to Abraham what He has spoken to him." Genesis 18:17-19

b. It is the prayer of the righteous

    "Let Your work appear to Your servants, and Your glory to their children. And let the beauty of the LORD our God be upon us, and establish the work of our hands for us; yes, establish the work of our hands." Psalms 90:16-17

Your faith in Christ should be the basic platform of your legacy.

""And these words which I command you today shall be in your heart. You shall teach them diligently to your children, and shall talk of them when you sit in your house, when you walk by the way, when you lie down, and

when you rise up. You shall bind them as a sign on your hand, and they shall be as frontlets between your eyes. You shall write them on the doorposts of your house and on your gates." Deuteronomy 6:6-9

"When I call to remembrance the genuine faith that is in you, which dwelt first in your grandmother Lois and your mother Eunice, and I am persuaded is in you also." 2 Timothy 1:5

A *Wedding Ceremony* in *Heaven*

"Then I heard what sounded like a great multitude, like
the roar of rushing waters and like loud peals of thunder,
shouting:
"Hallelujah!
For our Lord God Almighty reigns.
Let us rejoice and be glad and give him glory!
For the wedding of the Lamb has come, and his bride has
made herself ready.
 Fine linen, bright and clean,
was given her to wear."
(Fine linen stands for the righteous acts of the saints.)
Then the angel said to me, "Write: `Blessed are those who
are invited to the wedding supper of the Lamb!'"
Revelation 19:6-9

This therefore is your special invitation to the wedding supper of the Lamb.

But you need to receive your own fine linen, bright and clean: *"But when the king came in to see the guests, he noticed a man there who was not wearing wedding clothes. `Friend,' he asked, `how did you get in here without wedding clothes?' The man was speechless. "Then the king told the attendants, `Tie him hand and foot, and throw him outside, into the darkness, where there will be weeping and gnashing of teeth.' "For many are invited, but few are chosen"* Matthew 22:11-14

Therefore, if you want to become a true disciple of the Master-Jesus, so that He may qualify you and give you the wedding clothes for the marriage supper of the Lamb, please follow these guidelines (Acts. 2:37-47).

1.   Pray this prayer: Heavenly Father, I want to become your true child. Please forgive my sins (confess them) and let Your Holy Spirit come into my heart to make me a new creature. I believe and accept Jesus Christ, Your Son, as my LORD and Saviour. In Jesus name. Amen.

2. Get in touch with us: for more spiritual follow up.

3. A study of the CHRISFO Study Outlines (CSO) series on SALVATION will be of tremendous help to the genuineness of your foundations in Christ.

4. Get involved in any genuine Bible-believing gospel church near you.

5. Ensure that you register: for their foundation classes so that you can be baptized in water for the remission of your sins and can be properly discipled.

Knowing More About CHRISFO

A. INTRODUCTION

Christian Foundations (CHRISFO) is a non-denominational platform of collaboration with churches and Christian fellowships, organizations, etc. with a vision for the revival of genuine New Testament Christianity in the church and the fear of God in the land.

B. ACTIVITIES

Our activities are as follows:

1. Solemn Assembly:
A program aimed to encourage effective prayers with fasting for the well being of our nation and compatriots. This includes;

a. Solemn Assembly Conference; a period of about three days of anointed biblical expositions and teachings for the revival of New Testament Christianity. This may include tours.

b. National Prayer Meetings; arranging special prayer meetings, tours, etc. in response to unique developments in the nation or any part of it.

2. CHRISFO Affiliation

CHRISFO wants to work closely with you for the revival of New Testament Christianity and the fear of God in our land. Get in touch with us to collaborate.

C. STUDY MATERIALS:

1. CHRISFO STUDY OUTLINES (CSO):

Provide effective materials for Sunday School Outlines, House Fellowships, Bible Studies and other group and practical Bible discussions.

2. CHRISFO CDs: Seek to spread the effects of the Holy Spirit in the CHRISFO messages on the principles of genuine New Testament Christianity.

3. CHRISFO BOOKS:

Seek to present biblical expositions on the fundamental principles of genuine new testament Christianity.

4.   CHRISFO Tracts: are available for your distribution during evangelism, teachings and other gospel promotional endeavours.

D. CHRISFO BIBLE SCHOOL

The CHRSIFO Bible School is a platform of raising New Testament Christian ministers, who are approved unto God and rightly dividing the Word of Truth.

E.   CHINESE MINISTRY

We believe that the LORD has called CHRISFO to join in the evangelisation of Chinese people from different Asian countries that come into Africa. To facilitate this, CHRISFO has adopted a four action plan as follows:

1.   Raising prayer guard among ministers across denominations, who have a burden for the salvation of Chinese people.

2.   Giving the learning of Chinese language a prominent place in the CHRISFO Bible School.

3.   Seeking for and appropriating opportunities to use Chinese Language to preach the gospel

4.   Building Chinese Christian fellowships.

Contact us at:

SALVATION HOUSE,
1-3, Salvation Street, Off Pipeline Road,
Baale Akinosi, Ajuwon- Akute,
(via Ojodu Berger, Lagos)
Tel: 080 33011 351
E-mail: christianfoundations88@yahoo.com
web: www.chrisfo.org

CHRISFO Publications

On Marriage

On Salvation

CHRISFO Books (e-book and Paper Back Format) are available on
Amazon Books and **Okada Books**
Visit our website **chrisfo.com/books** for more details
or Contact us **+234 704 574 2908**

Other Titles

CHRISFO Books (e-book and Paper Back Format) are available on
Amazon Books and **Okada Books**
Visit our website **chrisfo.com/books** for more details
or Contact us **+234 704 574 2908**

CHRISFO STUDY OUTLINES (CSO)

www.ingramcontent.com/pod-product-compliance
Lightning Source LLC
Chambersburg PA
CBHW020926160726
47993CB00005B/2150